Greg Prince on His
Rights & LDS Chur

(Note this conversation was recorded on May 17, 2019 in Salt Lake City, Utah. I will use GT for Gospel Tangents to indicate when I am talking to Greg. The interview has been lightly edited to remove verbal miscues.)

Introduction

Welcome to Gospel Tangents. I'm your host Rick Bennett. Please consider donating or purchasing a transcript by going to our website https://GospelTangents.com/shop . You'll help support other documentaries and podcasts such as this.

I'm excited to have Historian Greg Prince on the show. Greg discusses his new book, "Gay Rights & the Mormon Church." We will discuss the political, legal and social reasons the LDS Church has used over the past few decades to define the relationship between the institution and gay church members. Check out our conversation....

Tags: Gospel Tangents, Rick Bennett, Latter-day Saints, LDS Church, Mormon, Mormon Church, Church of Jesus Christ of Latter-day Saints, Mormon history, Mormon, LDS, Church of Latter Day Saints, Greg Prince, Gay Rights, Mormon Church, gay LDS, gay Mormons, Gay Hawaii, Prop 8, Prop 22, DOMA, Defense of Marriage Act, LDS Church & Politics, Mormon Proposition, Hawaii LGBT, Methodist seminary, Methodist, Christian Right, Family Proclamation, Proclamation on the Family, revelation, whiplash, orthodox Mormons question, gay biology, Exclusion Policy,

Contents

Mixing Church & Politics in LGBT Fight

Introduction

I'm excited to have Greg Prince back on the show! We're going to talk about his new book, *Gay Rights and the Mormon Church* and we will discuss the history of LDS Church policy toward gays, and get into not only Prop 8 in California, but Prop 22 as well. We will also talk about the legal battles in Hawaii that led to federal legislation prohibiting gay marriage. But why did Greg write this book? He'll answer that in our next conversation….

Interview

GT 0:04 Welcome to *Gospel Tangents*. I have a fantastic guest, could you go ahead and introduce yourself?

Greg 0:10 I'm Greg Prince, just visiting Salt Lake from Maryland.

GT 0:14 That's right. So, it's great to have you here in Salt Lake, and thanks for coming on *Gospel Tangents*.

Greg 0:22 You're welcome.

GT 0:22 You're my first two time guest. So that's exciting. So, you've got a new book out. Tell us about your book.

Greg 0:30 The book is called *Gay Rights and the Mormon Church: Intended Actions, Unintended Consequences.*[1]

GT 0:36 Okay.

Greg 0:37 It came about very gradually, and I didn't realize for several years, what the initial catalyst was. It happened in the aftermath of Prop

---

[1] Can be purchased at https://amzn.to/2YOEvoE

8. In 2008, I was visiting my daughter who was a student at Boston University and I got a phone call from Helen Whitney. Helen, the prior year had produced a four-hour documentary called "The Mormons," which was broadcast on PBS.[2] So, I had gotten to know her over the course of two years in her preparing that documentary.

Greg 1:13 She said, "My best friend Andrew Solomon, who is a writer for *The New Yorker*, writer of some award winning books, has turned on me because of Prop 8." He said, "How could you have said anything nice in your documentary about this evil church that helped to pass Prop 8?" Then she asked if I could help to repair the friendship. That took a long time. We spent almost a year in occasional email correspondence trying to get the temperature down. Eventually, he agreed to do an article for *Dialogue*, but was involved in writing a monumental book called, *Far From the Tree*,[3] and so he never got around to doing the article. But I called him and said, "What if we do an interview instead?" So, I traveled to New York, spent an afternoon with him. That interview was published in *Dialogue*, and it's a remarkable interview.

Greg 3:02 Andrew could easily have just gone broadside against the church, and he could have attacked it for being a homophobic church. Although he didn't pull back completely, he certainly was critical of the church's actions, in that interview. He said, "I have achieved with my husband, John, a level of happiness that we didn't think was possible since we became legally married." Then he said, "I don't understand why the Mormon Church, or any church would want to deprive people of that level of happiness."

Greg 3:36 That was a very interesting way of putting it, and it caused me to start to rethink where I was. I was not homophobic, but I just was not aware of all of the nuances of the LGBTQ world. But that didn't drive me to write a book immediately. It was just the first in a series of things that pushed me in that direction. The second was when I came to know Rick

---

[2] Can be viewed at https://www.youtube.com/watch?v=uJyvEbnY9GQ
[3] Can be purchased at https://amzn.to/2Wu48Oa

Jacobs, almost by accident. Rick is a gay activist, lives in California, was the founder of a political action group called the *Courage Campaign*. In 2008 with Prop 8, that organization focused all of its efforts on trying to defeat Prop 8. When I met Rick, he quickly realized that I wasn't the stereotype of Mormons that he had thought. He said, "You're a reasonable guy." That began a friendship that lasts to this day, as does my friendship with Andrew Solomon. But both of them sensitized me to nuances that I had just not considered before.

Greg 4:47 Another pivotal event was when I was asked to join the board of directors of *Affirmation*. *Affirmation* has been around for over 30 years. It is an independent organization founded by LDS or former LDS gay men, but it's inclusive of the LGBTQ world, and in 2012 the newly elected president, Randall Thacker, reached out to me and asked if I would be on the board, saying that he wanted to turn the organization into one that built bridges, rather than burning bridges. For its history, prior to that time, *Affirmation* had mostly been an organization of older gay Mormon men who were yelling at the church. He changed that. I had a five-year stint on the board, it was an amazing opportunity to get to know at a very fundamental level, so many people with whom I would not have had contact otherwise.

Greg 5:35 So that gradual accumulation of knowledge, of associations, finally led me to the point where I thought, "There are stories here that haven't been told that need to be told." Initially, I thought I would write a book about Prop 8 and the Mormon Church's role in it. Because even though people knew that there had been a role, there had not been anything published that tried to take a comprehensive look at that. When I started with Prop 8, I quickly began to realize that Prop 8 wasn't told whole story. It reached backwards into Prop 22, which was similar legislation in California eight years earlier and that, in turn, was related to the Hawaii lawsuit that began in the early 1990s, which was really the first time when the courts took up the issue of marriage equality, in any serious fashion, enough so that people thought that that would be the turning point. They thought because of the way the lawsuit was progressing, that Hawaii would become the first state to legalize same sex marriage, and there was a national freak-out as a result, because of the full faith and credit clause of the U.S. Constitution. What is legal in one state must be accepted by other states and by the federal government, unless there are existing laws in those states or in the federal government, that would run to the contrary.

Greg 7:36 So as the Hawaii lawsuit progressed, you had a cascade of amendments to state constitutions, of state laws, of federal law, the Defense of Marriage Act, DOMA, directly resulted as a response to Hawaii. Everybody was freaking out that same sex marriage was somehow going to overtake the whole country. That's when the Mormon Church first decided to walk across the street, and rather than focusing its efforts inward, in other words, its relationship, its policies towards gay Latter-day Saints, it got into the public square, and became a major player in the Hawaii lawsuit and subsequent Hawaii legislation. But it didn't have a high profile there, primarily because it took great pains not to have one.

Greg 8:29 It created, with the Catholic Church, a front organization called *Hawaii's Future Today*, and unless you really knew where to look, you wouldn't have known that the church, at a very high level, meaning the First Presidency, Quorum of the Twelve and the Seventy, were operating substantially in Hawaii. It also didn't have as high profile because it was on the majority side of the issue. This is the 1990s. A strong majority of people throughout the country, were against same sex marriage. So it was riding the crest of a benevolent wave. The same thing happened in 2000 with Prop 22 in California. There was still a strong majority that was against same sex marriage.

Greg 9:28 When we got to 2008, what they didn't realize is that the sands had started to shift, that more people were rethinking their biases, and moving to the other side on the issue. But the other thing that had happened that was crucial with Prop 8 that the church didn't factor in, is that in earlier legal battles, the gays were trying to get something they'd never had. But when Prop 22 was struck down by the California Supreme Court, in the Spring of 2008, there was a window where gay couples in

7

California could be legally married, and tens of thousands were legally married. Then Prop 8 came in, and when it was passed, it took away something that they had owned. So, it was fundamentally different in that respect. From the earlier period, where these people were trying to get something they had never had, then they got it, then it was taken away. That changed the landscape enormously.

GT 10:05 Well, that's very interesting. So, it's funny how you you've gone from how did you get to writing the book to all these things back and I actually want to push back a little bit farther if we could. Because I know last night at *Benchmark Books* you had mentioned, Elder Oaks was kind of the architect and had a memo from, I believe it was 1984?

Greg 10:25 It was.

GT 10:27 Wasn't that the same year he was called it as an apostle?[4]

Greg 10:29 It was either the same year or shortly after that. It might have been 1983, I'm not sure.

GT 10:35 Okay.

Greg 10:35 But shortly after he became an apostle, and it was a fairly lengthy memorandum that became the playbook for the church, not just in the marriage equality issue, but in the overall treatment of LGBTQ people within the church.

GT 10:55 Can you tell us a little bit more about that then? What was the playbook there?

Greg 11:03 One fundamental issue within that playbook was that, "Look, we need to cast this as a moral issue, and not as a civil rights issue." Because he realized that if the public, including the public within the

---

[4] Oaks was called and sustained in General Conference in April 1984. Because he was a judge at the time of his call, he wasn't officially ordained until May 3, 1984. Incidentally, current President Russell M. Nelson was also called as an apostle in April 1984.

church, began to look at it as a basic civil rights issue, it would be an uphill slog for the church that they may not win. If they could paint it with morality paint, then they could carry the day much more easily, and that has been the playbook ever since and continues to be the playbook today.

GT 11:40 Isn't that the same playbook that the church used in the '50s and '60s with blacks?

Greg 11:45 Absolutely, it is.

GT 11:46 So does it feel like sometimes the church keeps making the same mistakes on these issues?

Greg 11:53 To me? Yes, and I think that the results of the last couple of decades would substantiate that.

The Christian Right & LGBT Fight

Introduction

Dr. Greg Prince serves on the Board of Directors for a Methodist seminary near Washington, D.C. It's not just the LDS Church that has had a difficult time dealing with gay rights. In our next conversation, we'll talk about how the Christian Right deals with gay rights, and specifically discuss what happened in the Prop 8 battle in California. Check out our conversation....

Interview

Greg 12:00 This has not been a series of victories for the church.

GT 12:07 It started out that way, though. Is that a fair statement?

Greg 12:12 When they walked across the street, they were on the winning side of Hawaii and they were on the winning side of Prop 22, and they won Prop 8, but were on the losing side.

GT 12:29 Won the battle but lost the war.

Greg 12:31 That's where it turned, because with the death of President Hinckley early in 2008, the church lost the man who probably best understood the P.R. value of this issue. His insistence had been, "We need to be in this battle, but we need to be in the background. We don't want to get out there in front, because that will have repercussions that we don't want." The church was able to follow that in Hawaii, and they followed it in California and some other states that had a much lower profile nationally. But then when he died, and the request came from the Catholic Church in California to have the Mormons join the coalition, Thomas Monson jumped on it immediately. And the church leaped in with both feet and took a profile that even though they tried to conceal the financial aspect of it by having church members donate money to a front organization, rather than having the church donate the money, the proposition came to be known as the Mormon Proposition.

GT 13:46 Okay, so let me make sure. Because I'm not super familiar with Prop 22, so as we're going through here, I want to make sure we're following timeline. So back in '84, Oaks puts forth this memo-- so what was going on in 84? Because in my mind, I don't think gay rights was a big issue back then.

Greg 14:05 It was not a big issue, but it was something that clearly was on his mind, and I think on the mind of some of his colleagues, and it was just, "Look, here's a position paper. Here's what we need to be thinking about in strategy as we move forward, because I think that these issues will achieve greater prominence, and we're going to have to deal with them."

GT 14:25 Was AIDS a big issue back then? I know, it was more in the late 80's.

Greg 14:29 Yes, it was. It was starting to blow up big time in the early 1980s, and that probably had something to do with his thinking on it.

GT 14:36 Okay.

Greg 14:36 Although it didn't deal a lot with the AIDS epidemic. So, you had that, the Hawaii lawsuit, which began in 1991, was the first time that marriage equality really took a serious hold on the national consciousness.

GT 14:53 Okay.

Greg 14:54 Then what Prop 22 in California did in 2000 was to embed in state law, a prohibition on same sex marriage.

GT 15:06 Oh, it put in a prohibition.

Greg 15:08 It put in a prohibition, but it did so as a state law.

GT 15:13 Okay.

Greg 15:15 Eight years later, after a series of lawsuits that were combined into one, the California Supreme Court struck down Prop 22, saying that it was unconstitutional per the California Constitution. So the proponents of Prop 22, were already gathering signatures for a proposition that had identical wording, but that was an amendment to the state constitution, rather than a state law. So if something is struck down as unconstitutional, if you can amend the Constitution, then it becomes de facto constitutional, and that was the whole point of Prop 8.

GT 16:02 Okay.

Greg 16:03 So it had a much different legal footing. Now, eventually, Prop 8 was challenged, not in California Court, because there would have been no standing to declare it unconstitutional, it was challenged in federal court and was struck down as being unconstitutional per the United States Constitution.

GT 16:26 Okay, so Prop 22 was declared unconstitutional, you said it was in about 2000?

Greg 16:33 No, it was passed in 2000. It was declared unconstitutional in May of 2008.

GT 16:42 Okay, then the follow up....

Greg 16:42 The pro-Prop 8 forces had already begun collecting signatures...

GT 16:47 Just in case ...

Greg 16:48 ....to put it on the ballot.

GT 16:51 Okay. So, between May and November, there were a significant number of gay marriages that occurred in California? Is that correct?

Greg 16:57 Tens of thousands, yes.

GT 16:58 Okay, so, by November, the church with a coalition of the Catholic Church and some other organizations--now, one of the things that I found interesting last night was you said that the Mormon Church combined with the Catholic Church combined with some evangelical organizations for some sort of a front organization, and then you said that they all said, "Well, we're behind you," but they weren't.

Greg 16:59 This went back to 2000, and it was reminiscent of Lucy and the football.

GT 17:34 Okay.

Greg 17:35 I won't lift up the football this time. And every time Charlie Brown fell for it, and every time she lifted up the football and he wound up on his back. So in 2000, the other churches said, "We're in this together," but the LDS Church wound up carrying all the water. In 2008, they said, "No, this time, we're really in this together," and the LDS Church wound up carrying most of the water. Because the money was given to a front organization, it's very difficult to figure out how large a role church members played in financing Prop 8. The best estimates are at least 50% of the $40 million, that the *Yes on 8 Movement* collected came from Latter-day Saints. It could have been substantially more than 50%, but we know that much just from reverse engineering because the donors' contributions were registered with the California Secretary of State, and a group of innovative church members looked at that list and started disseminating it to their network throughout the state, and identifying church members and then tabulating the amount of money collectively that hadn't been given by them.

GT 18:55 Oh, wow.

Greg 18:57 This is the main reason that it became known as the Mormon Proposition. The church also had a very impressive ground game going, where there were wards organized to do phone banks, to carry placards on the streets, to do door to door canvassing. Even the *No On 8* people had to acknowledge that this was a very, very impressive organization in the way that it was able to mobilize. But that just embedded more deeply in the public consciousness that this happened because of the Mormon Church, hence the Mormon Proposition, hence the immediate and sustained, and rather ferocious backlash against the church the day after Prop 8 passed.

GT 19:52 Is this just because the Mormons are better organized than evangelicals and Catholics? Or what do you think there?

Greg 19:58 Well, they certainly were better organized on this. The structure of the Mormon Church adapts very well to being mobilized on short notice. Usually, that's for very beneficial things like natural disasters. We were on the ground making a big difference in Katrina in New Orleans, before anybody else got there. So it's very impressive, but it can be used in a variety of directions, and in this case, the reaction I think caught leaders totally by surprise.

GT 20:38 So I'm curious about that, because it does seem like especially I know, abortion is kind of a big issue today, and it does seem like, and I'll just call it the Christian Right, which Mormons are sort of members, I guess. But it does seem like the Christian Right, especially with regards to abortion, is pretty well organized. Why doesn't that translate over to, say, Prop 8?

Greg 21:01 I don't know.

GT 21:05 Okay. I mean, I do know you mentioned a few times, in fact, the last time on our interview, that you're a member of the Board of Governors at a Wesleyan seminary there in D.C., is that right?

Greg 21:22 Yes.

GT 21:23 Can you update us on what's going on with the Methodist Church and gays?

Greg 21:26 The Methodists have a heap of trouble on this. In February of this year, they had what is termed a Called General Conference. They normally have general conferences once every four years. But they can have a special conference, and they did it for one issue, and that was LGBTQ. There were really three elements that they were considering

14

during this conference. One is how do we deal with religious talk about gays? Do we brand them as apostates? Do we brand them as sinners? The second was, will we allow the ordination of gay clergy? And the third was, will we allow the performing of gay marriages?

Greg 22:24 The conservatives prevailed, and that was primarily because of Africa. Forty-five percent of the delegates to the conference were from Africa, and that vote which was strongly homophobic, combined with the delegates from the American South prevailed, and it put the Methodist Church in a more homophobic stance than they had been prior to the conference. The other alternative that was put forward and voted down, was called the One Church proposal, and that was written primarily by the head of our Board of Governors. So, he was front and center in the debate, and he and other delegates from Wesley were just devastated with the outcome. It puts them in a much more difficult position, organizationally, than the LDS Church right now, because there's a very real possibility of permanent schism, that the United Methodist Church might not wind up being very united anymore. They're trying to work out some kind of a compromise that can avoid that, and when I went to the board meeting earlier this week, Tom looked at me and he said, "I never thought I'd see the day when the Methodists would make the Mormons look progressive."

GT 23:52 Well, that's interesting. So, the November Policy came out, which sounds like--is that is that where the Methodist church is right now is where the LDS Church was in 2015?

Greg 24:06 No, there are some fundamental differences in it. For instance, there has been no action on the part of the Methodists to say, "We declare these people in the state of Apostasy. They are subject to church discipline. We will not perform rites of passage on their children." Those are the elements of the November 2015 policy. It's different in saying--it mostly focused on the latter two of those three issues that I mentioned, the ordination of gay clergy, and the performing of same sex marriages. On the third one, we are in agreement right now institutionally with the Methodists.

15

GT 24:53 That we won't perform gay marriages.

Greg 24:54 The second one, we actually are in a more progressive stance now, because we do ordain openly gay clergy. Now we don't have a professional class of clergy. So, it's an all lay priesthood, but for more than a decade, we have sent openly gay missionaries, male and female on full-time proselytizing missions. So, we are indeed ordaining gay clergy, but it's different.

GT 25:30 As long as they're celibate.

Greg 25:32 As long as they're celibate, yes. But for the Methodists, that's not an option. They're saying no gay clergy.

GT 25:40 So, celibate or no, just period, if you declare you're gay. But do they have any clergy that have come out as gay after and do they get defrocked?

Greg 25:48 I don't know.

GT 25:48 You don't know. Okay. Yeah, that's interesting. So, it's just interesting to me to see how other groups are dealing with this issue, and I'm just really curious why this became the Mormon Proposition and not a Christian Right proposition, especially in California. Do you have any ideas on that?

Greg 26:17 It was because of the dominant role that the church played, both in fundraising, raising over half the total, and the church, I think, accounts for maybe 2% or 3% of the population in California, and they raised over 50% of the money. Then because of the ground game, they were out there in thousands, either on the streets, or manning phone banks, or doing door to door canvassing. They pretty much had an idea across the entire state of who was going to vote what. Part of the strategy was, for those who are leaning awards Prop 8, in other words, prohibiting gay marriage, we'll keep visiting them and encouraging them and making sure that they have arrived to the polls if they need it. For those who were leaning the other direction, we'll stay away from them.

GT 27:15 Well, it's just so funny to me, because it feels to me like, and I know abortion is kind of a hot issue right now, but it feels to me like the Christian Right is very organized on that issue. Why wouldn't that translate to this gay issue?

Greg 27:29 I don't know.

GT 27:31 It just seems strange to me.

Greg 27:33 But on the abortion issue, the LDS Church has tended to have a fairly progressive stance, that for years and years and years, we have carved out exceptions for rape, for incest, for the health of the mother, and those prevail to this day. The current legislation that's being passed in red states, doesn't allow for that. That's intentional, because they want to push this issue into the supreme court as quickly as they can, to try to overturn Roe vs. Wade. But the LDS Church has consistently maintained a position that even though it condemns abortion in principle, it has these important carve-ins.

GT 28:25 That's interesting.

Revelatory Whiplash

Introduction

When the Nov 2015 policy was announced, many LDS Church members were hurt to learn that children of gay parents couldn't be baptized, and gay couples were considered in apostasy. Fast forward to April 2019 and the policy was reversed, causing joy among some church members, and pain from other dues to the quick nature of the change. Still others were outraged at the reversal. Some church members may have felt whiplash at the sudden changes. Dr. Greg Prince will talk more about the pain caused by the Policy and its reversal. Check out our conversation....

Interview

GT 28:26 Let's talk a little bit about Hawaii. A lot of people, especially maybe heterosexual people aren't as familiar with this fight. Wasn't it this fight in Hawaii that also led to the Proclamation on the Family?[5]

Greg 28:45 It's hard to say that it led to it. I think that they were parallel tracks that eventually converge, but the one was not formulated specifically to assist the other. In December of 1993, gay couples in Honolulu went to the clerk and requested marriage licenses. They were turned down, as they expected. But on that basis, they subsequently filed the lawsuit challenging Hawaii law. They did it in the state courts because the Hawaii constitution is much more liberal regarding sex/gender issues than the U.S. Constitution. The district judge dismissed the case on summary judgment. It never went to trial.

Greg 29:31 But the plaintiffs appealed to the state supreme court, and when it went to the State Supreme Court, the justices there said, "Because of our Constitution, this case has to be tried under the legal doctrine of strict scrutiny." Whereas the judge at the district level had

---

[5] See https://www.lds.org/study/manual/the-family-a-proclamation-to-the-world/the-family-a-proclamation-to-the-world?lang=eng

dismissed it on the basis of what's called rational basis. Those are two levels of legal doctrine that govern how the courts respond to lawsuits challenging laws. Rational basis merely says the government can pass laws that people don't like, as long as there is a reasonable basis for doing so.

Greg 30:15 One of the easiest examples to think about is tax increases. Nobody likes tax increases, but if you go to court and challenge a tax increase, you're likely to lose because there is a compelling reason that the state needs to raise money. Strict scrutiny says if a law discriminates against a class of people, the state has the onus of proving to the courts that there is a compelling public interest that is being served, that justifies the discrimination. That's a lot of words. Example, many states, probably most states, have laws forbidding marriage of first cousins. Well, that's obviously a discriminatory law. It's putting a different standard to them than it does to the rest of population. But there is a compelling state interest because of health issues, that if you have first cousins marrying, you're going to have an increase in recessive genes that can be expressed, and a higher incidence of some fairly serious genetic and medical conditions. So those laws are allowed to stand.

Greg 32:33 When the Supreme Court sent the case back to the district court and said you must try this under strict scrutiny, then it became the burden of the state to prove that prohibiting gay marriage advanced the interest of the state, which meant they had to prove in a court of law under cross examination, that gay marriage was somehow damaging to the state. That had never happened before. So when that decision was handed down by the state Supreme Court, the ripple effect went all the way across the country and state after state immediately started to enact legislation, either laws or amendments to state constitutions, to try to set up the firewall, so that assuming, as everybody did, that the Hawaii lawsuit would result in the legalization of same sex marriage, states outside of Hawaii did not have to respect marriages that were performed in Hawaii if they involved same sex partners. The ripple effect reached the US capital as well and resulted in the DOMA the Defense of Marriage Act, which Bill Clinton was forced to sign because there was a veto proof majority in both houses.

GT 33:13 Okay. So that's how we got DOMA.

Greg 33:16 That's how we got DOMA and it was all an effort to block the ripple effect of the Hawaii lawsuit, because everybody assumed that that would be decided in favor of the plaintiffs, and ultimately, it was, but the other option going through the legislative process was then invoked in Hawaii, so that rather than dealing with the courts and the lawsuit, the church shifted gears and started to work on the legislative process, and eventually, there was a state amendment to the constitution that contravened the lawsuit.

GT 34:01 Okay, so that was passed in Hawaii.

Greg 34:04 Yeah, it was the same thing that later happened in California. There had been a law, the law was struck down by the courts, because it was unconstitutional, and then they fixed the Constitution. Same thing happened later in California with Prop 22, and Prop 8. In both cases, eventually, the federal courts struck both of those laws down saying that they are unconstitutional in light of the US Constitution.

GT 34:07 Okay.

Greg 34:13 Which always supersedes state constitutions if there are conflicts.

GT 34:35 So the *Family Proclamation* didn't really play a role as far as gay rights?

Greg 34:39 No, it played a very minor role. Twice, the church tried to intervene in the court case and become a co-defendant, because church leaders felt that the Hawaii Attorney General would not mount a robust defense of the existing law. The first time they were smacked down at the district court level, which said you have no standing in this. Then a couple of years later, they appealed that to the state Supreme Court, but they were turned down again. The brief that they filed the second time, which was in 1996, included, in its appendix, the *Proclamation on the Family*, which had been rolled out by the church the prior year. But it was not written specifically to advance the church's cause in the Hawaii case. It was much broader in its intended effect. But yeah, it was borrowed at that point, but it was a minor thing. It was a footnote.

GT 35:45 Okay. So why was the proclamation put out then? Because I've always thought it was to deal with, a child should be raised with a man and a woman as a parent...

Greg 35:58 It's not been clear to me what the 1, 2, 3 steps were in getting it started. I know that there were professors at the BYU Law School, who had a hand in some of the early drafts of it. Kirton-McConkie, the law firm that does much of the church's legal work, had a hand in it. It went back and forth with the Q15.[6] I think that there was a realization that in order to have, not just standing in the courts, but in order to draw a line for church members, that there was a need to define what the church felt the family was. Most of the *Proclamation on the Family* is positive, I would say at least 90% of it. But the other part is not positive, and it clearly is lashing out and staking out a position against gay marriage. Now, there's an interesting phrase in there, such that if the church ever were to take a different position, it could grab that, and it says gender is eternal. That can cut either direction, depending on how you want to define it. So we'll see.

GT 37:20 Well, that's kind of a nice little segue into Mormon theology as far as gender. Can you just talk a little bit about Mormon theology, especially as it relates to same sex marriage?

Greg 37:40 I think that our position as a church effectively represents a reverse engineering of an afterlife theology. Because LDS afterlife theology does not recognize gay. So, if it does not, then if you reverse engineer that into the present, you say, well, if it can't exist there, then

---

[6] Quorum of the Twelve and First Presidency.

it's not legitimate here. That leads to the behavioral paradigm of homosexuality. Look, there is no legitimate state of homosexuality. So, this is just a temporary, chosen thing, and you can choose yourself out of it. So, buck up and start acting manly, because most of the focus has been on gay men in the church, not on women.

Greg 38:38 But if you dig deeper into LDS theology, particularly going back into the first decade of the church's existence, you see that afterlife theology went through a substantial evolutionary process, that where we are now is not where we started, and that begs the question, are we at a permanent stopping point, or using the phrase from one of our *Articles of Faith*, is there yet to be revealed something else? I don't know the answer to that, but I don't have a closed mind about it either, both because we have that fundamental doctrine of continuing revelation, which means continuing change, and because historically, you can look back and see how that and every other significant doctrine in the church has changed somehow, at some point since 1830.

GT 39:37 Yeah, I know we talked a little bit about that last time, and I think that was one of the great quotes that you said was, "There's no doctrine that hasn't changed significantly."[7]

Greg 39:45 I've yet to see one, and I have yet to have somebody point one out to me. I'll qualify that by saying a significant doctrine. Who knows what little tidbits here or there that we've ignored? I haven't seen one yet.

GT 40:01 Well, you know, another thought is, I know the last time when I talked to you, we had the November policy in place and that was removed a few days before General Conference.

Greg 40:12 Yeah.

---

[7] See https://gospeltangents.com/2017/12/ailing-church-leaders-not-ideal-governance/

GT 40:12 I know, some people made an interesting observation last night at your book signing, that there was not a single mention of that [in General Conference]. Why do you think that was?

Greg 40:25 I think that's because they had good input from Public Affairs, that if you're going to announce something like that, which is not real cheery news for the institution, because you're erasing something that people thought was permanent, when you called it a revelation three years earlier. The way to do it, essentially, is what the government does when it has bad news. You announce it after five o'clock on a Friday afternoon, so that by Monday, people have pretty much moved on. By announcing it a couple days before General Conference, and then not mentioning it, it became non-news. I think that was a good move on their part.

GT 41:08 So, I know a lot of people, I know that I was very happy with the announcement. But I know a lot of people have been just as upset, and I think the main reason why is because there was no apology. I know Elder Oaks is often quoted as, "The church doesn't apologize."[8] Do you think it would have been a Public Relations win if the church had said we know there's been some damage done here, or do you agree with Elder Oaks, "The church just doesn't apologize."

Greg 41:45 No, I don't agree with that. I think they should apologize on multiple things, and it would have been a P.R. win, if they had said humbly, "We apologize for the damage that this has done," because demonstrably it did a lot of damage. Families were ripped apart. I think there's good evidence that more than a few people took their lives over this, and you can't undo that by reversing the policy. That's the real residual damage of this thing. It's not like okay, we went there, now we've come back, now let's go on and life goes on as it did before, but it doesn't. You step in something and you step out of it, but you still got it in your shoes, and that's where we are? How do you undo that kind of damage? It also creates a dilemma that may even affect the orthodox church member

---

[8] See https://archive.sltrib.com/article.php?id=2122123&itype=cmsid

more than the progressive church member, and that is, "Wait a minute, you told us this was revelation, and now three years later, you're saying it's back to where we were?" That creates a real dilemma.

GT 43:01 I have actually seen some orthodox members say, "I think the church is now in apostasy."

Greg 43:07 Yes. It's an unforced error, but, nonetheless, it's something that they're going to have to deal with, and it has repercussions because it affects the whole brand of revelation. If people thought that something being called revelation conferred permanence to it, now it becomes much more relative, and it has a ripple effect beyond that particular revelation. It calls into a question other [revelations] and say, "Well, how unchangeable is the rest of it?" In my mind, changeability is bedrock for Mormonism, but it's something that makes most church members really nervous. They will embrace the concept of continuing revelation, but they're really hesitant to accept change. It's a paradox.

GT 44:06 Well, you know, I've seen some people comment, and I would love to have you comment on this. You know, there's the story of Aaron and the golden calf. When the Israelites came through, and Moses was up in the mountain, and Aaron acquiesced to the sinful nature of the people and gave them a golden calf. I know that there are some orthodox members that that use that as a parallel with this policy, and say, "Well, maybe the members are so sinful, and the leaders are giving us what we want as a people." How would you respond to that analogy?

Greg 44:48 I don't know how to respond to it. I don't agree with that assessment. The whole dilemma that leaders of any religious movement have to deal with is how do you tap into the divine will and make that accessible to your members? It's not an easy thing to do. How do you discern the will of God and then translate that into action, into policy, into attitude? Does God change over time, or do we change? Do we vary in our ability to discern what that will is? Those are big questions, and there's no easy answer for them. I don't have an answer. But I think that it certainly says that there's constant struggle or needs to be, as leaders of any religious movement try to discern and make available to their believers that divine will.

Legal, Science, and Social Issues on LGBT

Introduction

What are some of the legal, science, and social reasons the LDS Church may have removed the Policy of Exclusion? Greg Prince answers these questions. Check out our conversation….

Interview

GT 45:58 I know in our last interview, one of the things that, what's the word? The people that disagreed with you the most, I guess we'll put it that way. Previously, we had talked,[9] and I know it came up again last night, where you had said that it was a straw man, where people think that the government will now force gay marriages. You'd given an example, has a rabbi ever been forced to marry a Jew and Gentile and things like that? So, I know there are still some people, if you look at my comments, I have a few lawyers that say that your argument is a straw man.

Greg 46:44 I base my argument on two bits of data. One is that when the Hawaii decision was handed down, that invalidated the law, the Hawaii Supreme Court made it explicit, that under no circumstances would the LDS Church or any church be required by the state to perform any kind of marriage, that the authority to perform marriages resided in the state. It could be given to churches and give them the privilege of performing marriages that would be legal, but there was no obligation that extended with that privilege. In other words, the state could not say, "Here's how you have to do it. Here's who you have to perform ceremonies for." It was made explicit in that. The other data point is lengthy conversations with Bill Eskridge, who is a professor of law at Yale. He is considered the

---

[9] See our previous interview: https://gospeltangents.com/2017/11/10/nothing-lds-theology-justifies-whacking-infants/

top legal expert in the country on LGBTQ law. He said and in fact wrote an op-ed for the Salt Lake Tribune to this effect, "It isn't going to happen." The Constitution is absolutely clear that by the separation of church and state, the state cannot dictate to any church, what marriages they need to perform. It can say you can't perform certain types. For instance, it would frown on churches trying to conduct plural marriages, because there's a national law against it. But it cannot intervene and say you must perform this kind of marriage or we will take away your tax exemption." It's just not there.

GT 48:38 Well, let me ask you about this. Just recently, we've had the change in LDS weddings, which I think has been a welcome change for a lot of people. I think this came up last night as well. How much of that was a social issue and how much did it have to do with gay marriage, the separation of sealing from an actual marriage?

Greg 49:03 It's a good question, and I don't have any information that allows me to answer it. What it did was to put countries around the world on essentially the same footing. Most countries have not allowed LDS temple weddings to be the wedding of record. They hold that that authority resides only with the state, and no religious institution is granted that authority. So in most countries, it's been the law all the way along, that if an LDS couple want to get married in the temple, they go to the clerk first. They have the legally authorized wedding, and then they go to the temple for what then becomes a temple sealing. So, this puts the U.S. now on the same footing as the other countries. It also puts the U.S. back to where it was until the late 1960's. At that point, you could get married anywhere and the same day or the next day or the next week, go to the temple and have a sealing and everything was fine. But somebody decided in the late '60s, that didn't do that anymore, that somehow the civil marriage degraded the value of the temple, and so they said, "No, if you want a temple marriage, you need to do that without a civil one, and if you get a civil one, first, we're going to make your wait a year until you can get a temple sealing."

27

GT 50:33 Yeah. So, for those maybe conservative legal scholars that think that there was a problem with the government forcing a gay wedding in a temple, do you think that this policy will assuage those fears be because it has now separated the two?

Greg 50:52 It could have been a factor in their thinking, and certainly, if that were ever to be a case, it gives them an escape. But I'm not an attorney. I'm not an authority on legal issues. I speak as one who has spoken to people who are authorities, particularly to Bill. If those attorneys who disagree, want to get into the dialogue, they should get into a dialogue with him and not me.

GT 51:21 Alright.

Greg 51:24 If they want to talk science, I can talk that.

GT 51:27 Well, that's something that we haven't talked about. Let's talk a little bit about the science, because I do know that we've changed. I know, President Kimball had a big book *Miracle of Forgiveness*[10], and I believe that's a chapter in your book?

Greg 51:43 Yes.

GT 51:44 Can you talk a little bit about that, and how the church has changed?

Greg 51:47 Well, the church, along with, really American society for decades, when they first started to view homosexuality as different and a threat and evil and even criminal, the basis of that was that this is a chosen behavior that goes contrary to society. So, it was a behavioral paradigm, not that you're born this way. We've had a lot of people in society and a lot of men in church leadership, who have come right out over the years and said, "The whole idea that you could be born this way is heresy. God would never do that." Biology had not even spoken on the issue yet, because it didn't have the tools.

---

[10] See https://amzn.to/2W9fCXM

Greg 52:42 Decades ago, researchers started looking at twins to see if that gave them clues as to the cause of homosexuality. If it were strictly genetic, then identical twins would always be the same. If one were gay, the other would be gay, if one were straight, the other would be straight. Fraternal twins, because they don't share the same genetic makeup would be expected to be different, like maybe not concordant at all. It turned out that it was a mixture of the two, that with identical twins, the concordance would be in the neighborhood of 50 to 60%--one twin is gay, then it would be likely that the other also would be gay, but not essential. Whereas with fraternal twins, it was maybe around 20%. So what that really said, although we didn't realize the ramifications of it at that time was, genetics is part of it, but there's something else that's part of it, and we didn't know what to call that yet. Eventually, that came to be known as epigenetics, which are factors that work on how the genes function, but they're not the genes themselves.

Greg 53:56 The other thing that predated molecular biology was the birth order effect, and it only functions in males. When a woman has a male child, there is whatever the percent is chance that that boy will be gay. It may be 5%, maybe 10%, we really don't know, but it's somewhere in that neighborhood. For the next son, the probability of that son being gay goes up 33% from his older sibling. Female births have nothing to do with this. It doesn't affect females, and they don't affect the male birth order effect. But, if you have multiple male births, it's additive. So with each subsequent birth, the probability of that boy being gay is 33% higher than with his older sibling. That was known for a long time. With the advent of molecular biology, and with sophisticated studies now about all of the factors that can influence how genes express themselves, we have seen much more of an effect of epigenetics and how it is the force that results in sexual preference and gender identity. Now, those two things, sexual preference being who do I go to bed with? Gender identity being who do I go to bed as? Everybody has both of those. The majority would be heterosexual in their sexual preference and cisgender, meaning that their identity matches their anatomy.

Greg 55:59 Well, put those on a grid, and you can see that you've got multiple possibilities, particularly when you start to realize that there are more than one or two options on either axis there. So, it becomes very complicated. We haven't even defined yet, all of the different flavors of what now more and more is becoming known as non-heterosexuality. Because homosexuality doesn't describe everything that's not heterosexual. There are things in between, like bisexual, and asexual and intersex where somebody actually has biological components of both sexes. So, it's very complicated. There will be no one-size fits all, to explain how somebody developed in this direction, versus that direction. But it is becoming clearer with time that this is biology. It's an imprint deep within the fetal brain that is present at birth, and it's permanent, and you can't change it.

Greg 57:06 So gradually, as science has spoken louder and louder, you have the fading of the behavioral paradigm and replacement by the biological paradigm. That's a difficult transition for a lot of people to make. It's a difficult transition for a lot of institutions to make, and even though the LDS Church is partially there, in that it said in its website Mormonsandgays.org, "It's not a choice." They're hedging their bets, because essentially, they're saying, "Who you are, even though you didn't choose to be that, you're not allowed to be. You can't act out what you are biologically, or we will punish you." That's where we are right now, and I don't think that's a sustainable policy. But that transition from the behavioral paradigm to the biological paradigm is a work in progress, and it will be a slow work. But science, I can assure you will speak more and more clearly on this. The problem is, there are so many different flavors out there. Each one is likely to have a different biological process underpinning it, and so defining each one of those, is going to take a long time.

GT 58:32 Interesting. All right. Well, the last question I have for you that I just wanted to address here, I know last night, I believe you said that, as a result of the November 2015 policy, do you have any sense for how many people left the church?

Greg 58:50 I have heard, I think from solid authority, that in the year following the announcement of the policy, over 60,000 people..

GT 58:58 In one year..

Greg 58:59 ...resigned their church membership formally, and you would have to figure that more people would be likely just to walk away than to go through the process of writing the letter to have their name removed. So, do the arithmetic there. It may be into the hundreds of thousands. I don't know. I don't know if the church knows, because for those who just disappear, how do you know what the reason was, if they just quietly walk away?

GT 59:28 Because that Jana Riess, right?[11]

Greg 59:29 Because if you have enough people quietly walking away, it's not quiet anymore, it's thundering, and I've just got to think that that weighed into their decision to eliminate that policy. Otherwise, why would they reverse ground? Especially when they called it revelation? That's a tough corner to get out of, but they got out of it.

GT 59:52 Do you have a sense? Is that why they reversed the policy?

Greg 59:56 I don't know.

GT 59:59 Okay. Are we going to get those people back?

Greg 1:00:03 I doubt it, because those who have left that I've spoken to or that I've heard about, generally were angry when they left, and if they're angry when they leave, you're not likely to get them back. That's the very sad part, and that's why just reversing the policy didn't get us back to where we were before we had the policy. A lot of damage has been done, and I think most of it can never be undone.

---

[11] Jana Riess and Ben Knowlton created a scientific survey on Mormons and ex-Mormons and she found reasons why people left the LDS Church. Jana will discuss her research in a future interview here at *Gospel Tangents*.

GT 1:00:32 All right. Well, do you have any last thoughts you want to share with our group? Where can we get your book?

Greg 1:00:40 You can get it on Amazon.[12] I know that. That's probably the best place to go because they're giving a fairly deep discount on it.

GT 1:00:48 Okay. All right. Well, Greg, Prince, I really appreciate you spending so much time here talking on *Gospel Tangents*.

Greg 1:00:55 My pleasure.

GT 1:00:56 Thanks.

---

[12] See https://amzn.to/2YOEvoE

Additional Resources:

Kurt Francom on Church Leadership & Culture

Kurt Francom of Leading Saints podcast tells how he is trying to help LDS leaders create better culture around church history, faith transitions, and being LGBT friendly.

223: Do You Disagree with the Exclusion Policy?
https://gospeltangents.com/2018/12/03/disagree-exclusion-policy/

222: Should the Church Modify Bishop's Interviews?
https://gospeltangents.com/2018/11/30/church-modify-bishops-intvws/

221: Results of Faith Crisis Research
https://gospeltangents.com/2018/11/27/results-faith-crisis-research/

220: "We've Got to Have These Difficult Conversations"
https://gospeltangents.com/2018/11/24/we-must-have-difficult-conversations/

219: Ministering to the Faithful & Faithless
https://gospeltangents.com/2018/11/20/ministering-to-the-faithful-faithless/

218: Is it Bad to be Called LDS or Mormon?
https://gospeltangents.com/2018/11/18/is-it-bad-to-be-called-lds-or-mormon/

Final Notes

You can get our transcripts at our amazon.com author page. I've got a link here, but just do a search for Gospel Tangents interview, and you should be able to find a bunch of them there. Please subscribe at Patreon.com/gospeltangents. For $5 a month, you can hear the entire interview uncut and for $10 you can get a pdf copy. We've also got a $15 tier where if you want a physical copy, I'll be the first to send it to you, so please subscribe at Patreon or on our website at Gospeltangents.com. For our latest updates, please like our page at facebook.com/Gospeltangents and also check our twitter updates Gospel tangents. Please subscribe on our apple podcast page tinyurl.com/GospelTangents, or you can subscribe on your android device. Just do a search for Gospel Tangents. Thanks again for listening. Click here to subscribe, here for transcript and over here we've got some more of our great videos. Thanks again.

Made in the USA
Las Vegas, NV
19 November 2021

34837349R00021